THE RAPTURED SAINTS

AND THE LEFT BEHIND

ISABEL RADEBE

SWEETSPIRE LITERATURE
—— MANAGEMENT ——

CONTENTS

THE 1ˢᵀ COMING OF CHRIST

The purpose of this Coming was to introduce the Kingdom of GOD and of Heaven to all creation. To open a way for the Gospel of the Kingdom that is now Preached to all Nations.

It is the truth as it is written in John 14:6 that JESUS CHRIST (the Anointed ONE) is the only way and the truth and the life. No one comes to the Father except through HIM. HE HIMSELF told Nicodemus (the one who came to HIM asking how to be saved) that unless one is born again, he cannot see the kingdom of God. I have written a book about Salvation and receiving the HOLY SPIRIT and as well as the previous book tittle "JESUS is Coming" for further details on salvation subject. Through salvation, to enter this Kingdom, man needs to be saved through CHRIST alone, as written in the book of Romans 10:9-11, where it speaks of the Good News of Salvation. We then read in Revelation 20:11-15 that one day the dead, both great and small, will stand before the judgement seat of GOD's throne. The books will be opened, including the

Book of Life, and the dead will be judged according to their deeds, as recorded in the books. In John 5:25 JESUS has warned us that, a time is coming and has now come when the dead will hear the voice of the Son of GOD and those who hear will live. Also time will come when the sea will give up its dead, and the death and the grave would also give up their dead, and all would be judged according to their deeds. Then death and the grave would be thrown into the lake of fire. This lake of fire is said to be the second death which was not meant for men, but for fallen angels and Satan. Due to man's defiance to receive salvation freely from GOD's Grace, anyone whose name is not found recorded in the Book of Life will be thrown into the lake of fire.

During HIS first Coming, Simeon saw GOD's Salvation where he said JESUS is the Savior of all humankind. I would like to close this Preface by quoting the words mentioned by the Prophet Simeon in Luke 2:25-35 when JESUS was presented to the Temple where he said:

> 25"And behold, there was a man in Jerusalem whose name
> was Simeon, and this man was just and devout, waiting for the
> Consolation of Israel, and the HOLY SPIRIT was upon him. 26And
> it had been revealed to him by the HOLY SPIRIT that he would
> not see death before he had seen the Lord's Christ. 27So he came by
> the Spirit into the temple. And when the parents brought in the

> Child Jesus, to do for Him according to the custom of the law,
> 28he took Him up in his arms and blessed GOD and said:

> 29"Lord, now You are letting Your servant depart
> in peace, According to Your Word;

30For my eyes have seen Your salvation

31Which You have prepared before the face of all peoples,

32 A light to bring revelation to the Gentiles,
And the glory of Your people Israel."

33 And Joseph and His mother marvelled at
those things which were spoken of Him.

34Then Simeon blessed them, and said to Mary His mother,
"Behold, this Child is destined for the fall and rising of
many in Israel, and for a sign which will be spoken against
35(yes, a sword will pierce through your own soul also),
that the thoughts of many hearts may be revealed.

The Scripture in Matthew 3 opens with words spoken by the voice of the one who was crying in the wilderness, John the Baptist, preparing the way of the LORD JESUS and making HIS paths straight. John preached a central message to multitudes saying,

"Repent: for the kingdom of heaven is at hand."

Again, in Matthew 4:17, we read that JESUS, being full of the HOLY GHOST, began HIS ministry with a powerful preaching of this central message saying,

"Repent: for the kingdom of heaven is at hand."

As I related in one of my dreams, the LORD JESUS appeared in human form, preaching the Good News of the Kingdom, saying,

> *"Repent: for the kingdom of heaven is at hand."*

It is also written in Luke 4:43 that when JESUS began HIS ministry, the crowd in Galilee tried to keep HIM from leaving them and HE said to them,

> *"I must preach the Kingdom of GOD to the other cities also, because for this purpose I have been sent."*

In the book of Acts, we find the same message which was preached to multitudes. Even today, the same message about HIS Kingdom is preached universally through the Ministry of the HOLY SPIRIT, saving many souls. The Kingdom of Heaven has already come into the hearts of people as we also witness many people receiving the gift of salvation and their lives being changed.

In the Acts of the Apostles, under the power of the HOLY SPIRIT, Phillip and Paul also preached the Gospel of the Kingdom and its blessings. It is all about JESUS and HIS righteousness in re-establishing the Kingdom that will never be shaken but will last forever (Hebrews 12:28). From the above scriptures, we can see that the preaching of the Kingdom was always under the divine mission of the power of the HOLY GHOST because this preaching is about the establishment of GOD's rule in this world as it is in Heaven. In Luke 17:21, JESUS said the Kingdom of Heaven is within us because JESUS CHRIST is already reigning in the hearts of the believers whilst the Kingdom of GOD was always in existence and is eternal.

The conclusion is that, every person must belong to either the Kingdom of GOD or the kingdom of darkness. JESUS is the KING and LORD of all nations and kingdoms (Revelation 19:16) but in the kingdom of darkness, Satan is the leader. In the book of Colossians 1:13, Paul says, "GOD has delivered us from the power of darkness and has translated us into the kingdom of HIS dear Son".

There is a Gospel of Salvation for individuals, where JESUS is the King in your heart through the work of the HOLY SPIRIT and the Gospel of the Kingdom for all nations. If one does not receive JESUS as his or her LORD and Savior, you will not enter HIS Kingdom. You will be in the kingdom of darkness where there is no light.

I have learned through the Work of the HOLY SPIRIT that JESUS and the Apostle of the early church were not preaching the Gospel of only love but the Gospel of love and REPENTANCE because the world has sinned against GOD. They emphasized on REPENTANCE and your signs will be forgiven. JESUS HIMSELF was preaching about REPENTANCE to enter HIS Kingdom. When JESUS went back to heaven, HE left us with the HOLY SPIRIT to guide and lead us as it is written in the book of John 16:8-13. It is my prayer that as the HOLY SPIRIT is restoring the church to do the works as the early church did, we must also preach the correct Gospel of love and REPENTENCE for Salvation of Souls since this is scriptural and not any other way – I have now understood the Apostolic Message of Salvation more than before. REPENTANCE is critical for entering into HIS Kingdom and not come as you are Gospel preached today. I have learned the order of preaching the Good News of Salvation through the BLOOD of JESUS as once off scarified for all, and then lead people to:-

- Repent and your sins will be forgiven;
- Receive Salvation by Grace (believing that JESUS has died for our sins and we are sinners);
- Be baptised with water and receive the HOLY SPIRIT;
- Once you have received the HOLY SPIRIT, HE will help to sanctify until one becomes like JESUS in characte

As JESUS is Coming Ministry, we now follow the above Apostolic order which is scriptural. Sometimes where there is no River Jordan near us to Baptized, we just use a big bath to Baptize the newborn again. By following the Apostolic order that is there in the book of Acts as the HOLY SPIRIT is restoring the church, we see the greatest move of the HOLY SPIRIT and many new believers being added to the Kingdom of God.

THE RAPTURE OF SAINTS

Just before Rapture JESUS mentioned that there will be falling away and just before the Son of Man comes, it will be like it was in the days of Noah. For in the days before the flood, people were eating and drinking, marrying and giving in marriage, up to the day Noah entered the ark; and they knew nothing about what would happen until the flood came and took them all away. These falling away conditions are also written in the book of 2 Timothy 3:1-5, lets read this scripture and see if we are already living in the End of End Times:-

"But mark this: There will be terrible times in the last days. 2 People will be lovers of themselves, lovers of money, boastful, proud, abusive, disobedient to their parents, ungrateful, unholy, 3 without love, unforgiving, slanderous, without self-control, brutal, not lovers of the good, 4 treacherous, rash, conceited, lovers of pleasure rather than lovers of God— 5 having a form of godliness but denying its power (denying the HOLY SPIRIT). Have nothing to do with such people."

I believe we all agree that we are already in the End of the End Times or the Last Days. Apart from the above scriptures, in Psalm 102:13 we read that Zion (what is happening in Israel today) is the clock to the End Times. The war between Israel – Palestine started in the ancient times including the times of King David-Goliath wars, Samson-Philistinian wars, Soul-Jonathan being killed in the same land, and these wars happened to times when Judea (which was the holy land during JESUS Times) was destroyed and the Rome renamed it as Palestinia after JESUS ascension. The above wars continued till to date as it happened in the ancient times but the difference is that we now see the apocalypse or final wars triggered by the same two sides that are mentioned in the book of Revelation and the prophecies of the End Times. In the book of Daniel, we read that a ruler coming from one of these two sides:- will do the following-

> *"He will confirm a covenant with many for **one 'seven.'** In the middle of the 'seven' he will put an end to sacrifice and offering. And at the temple he will set up an abomination that causes desolation, until the end that is decreed is poured out on him."*

The Quran 8 61 also agrees that there will be a seven-year peace covenant signed between Israel-Palestine.

The peace covenant to be signed is in the news all over the world today. One can ask a question, is GOD saying something about the apocalypse of today that will lead to the above seven years covenant? It was on the day when Israel was about to celebrate the Simchat Torah (the joy of the LORD) on the 7th to the 8th of October 2023 as it is described in the book of Deuteronomy 16 that there should be rejoicing in the festival of booths. As we were discussing with another Jewish Descended African Prophetess, the revelation received was that, an important celebration supposed to glorify the GOD of Abraham, our GOD, the Almighty, the Chief Shepherd and the ONE who has made the Heaven and the Earth but instead the celebration grieved GOD since it was not done to glorify GOD. Sukkot, as an example *(which is the feast of Tabernacles leading to the promised of the Messianic Age Celebration when all nations will be flowing to Jerusalem to worship the LORD)* is another critical celebration that is like a shadow to the future Sukkot *since* Jerusalem will be the Capital City of the whole World when CHRIST Rheign with HIS Saints. All prophecies reveal that there won't be peace in this land until JESUS, (the PRINCE of Peace) Second Coming. The wedding of the Bride and the Torah (Word), represent JESUS HIMSELF. The bride in this case is supposed to be dancing with the Word (JESUS) as in John 1 under future Sukkot. This was not done as in the book of Deuteronomy 16 to dance for the joy of the LORD, but it was celebrated in an ungodly manner.

The 1st Sabbath of October 2023 was also the 50th Sabbatical Year of 2023 Jubilee after the Jubilee of 1973 where on the 6th to the 26th of October 1973 the same violence interrupted between the two states which extended to other states. In the whole bible, whenever Israel ignore GOD's ways and choose their religious ways, they were caught by surprise since from the ancient times. The only thing that kept them in existence for years is the Covenant that GOD has made with Abraham as HE chose them as HIS own.

I have started by saying in Psalm 102:13 Zion is the clock to the End of the End Times. Daniel says the last apocalypse will lead to the signing of the peace covenant with terms and conditions for this covenant it to last for seven-years but in the middle of this one seven, it will be broken because in Daniel 2 the feet (nations of 8 61 above) are of the mixture of clay and iron which is a league that will not last for a long time (Psalm 83 reveals the names of the league and in this apocalypse we see the same states mentioned there since all prophecies are truth). The league of Psalm 83 has never come together as a league in the ancient times except today in these End Time. Prophet Daniel said in the middle of the week, a great tribulation will happen and in the book of 1 Thessalonians 5:5, the scripture gives us an assurance that, we (the CHRIST Followers) are all children of the light and children of the day. We do not belong to the night or to the darkness (wrath). GOD did save Noah's and Lot's beloved ones and HE will still save us from the tribulation hour only if we trust in HIM and HIS WORD. In John 10:35 we are told that, God's Word is truth; what He says is true. We cannot simply discard it this truth because we disagree with it. If we do, we are, in effect calling GOD a liar.

Brothers and sisters know that Rapture will happen at any time; we must always be ready since there is no prophecy that is not yet fulfilled for the Rapture to happen. "I better be ready, and CHRIST does not come - rather not to be ready, and HE comes". This is because HE will not come twice but once for only those who are ready. The church dispensation period is written in the bible from the book of Acts 1 to Revelation 3 only, and we are now living in the days of Revelation.

Apart from different interpretations of scriptures, anyone who follows JESUS' Commands will be Raptured. So, whether you believe in the pre- or post-Rapture, the important thing is to be obedient and follow HIS Commands. We read Paul telling the Thessalonians that,

16"For the Lord Himself will descend from heaven with a shout, with the voice of an archangel, and with the trumpet of God. And the dead in CHRIST will rise first. 17Then we who are alive and remain shall be caught up together with them in the clouds to meet the Lord in the air. And thus, we shall always be with the Lord." - 1 Thessalonians 4:16-17

In other words out of today's living population of about 7,963,000,000 billion *(PRB Mid-2022 Population Stats)*, those who are saved by faith in CHRIST will be caught-up. In out of about 117,020,448,575 billion of our species have ever been born on Earth, those who believed but died their graves will open up and they will be raised to meet with those alive on air to meet with the LORD. Depending on HIS Coming Time.

JESUS said we must all,

" Watch therefore, and pray always that you may be counted worthy to escape all these things that will come to pass, and to stand before the Son of Man." - Luke 21:36-37

Hebrews 12:22-23 says,

"22 But you have come to Mount Zion, to the city of the living God, the heavenly Jerusalem. You have come to thousands upon thousands of angels in joyful assembly,

23 to the church of the firstborn, whose names are written in heaven."

In John 14, the believers or followers of CHRIST will be taken to HIS FATHER's dwelling place in heaven which is the place of habitation, and it is in the heavenly city of Jerusalem where Luke 21:36 mention that it as a place to escape the great tribulation by grace for a short while before HIS Second Coming. The greatest sign of HIS Coming before Rapture is the FALLING AWAY that we see today even from HIS followers just like in the days of Noah (Matthew 24:37-39).

In April 2010, I had a dream where I saw people being Caught-up or Raptured into the air (they were taken very quickly). This happened during the day where again we were busy with our daily activities. When this happened, again I was outside the house and suddenly I saw people being caught up or pulled very quickly, separated from others who were left on the earth. It came to my mind in the dream that the pulling power was the power of the HOLY SPIRIT HIMSELF.

This pulling power was a visible snatching-up (like a fast wind) and these people were pulled up to the sky in the twinkling of an eye as it happened. The last person I saw being taken just next to where I stood, was a woman in her mid-sixties holding a baby. I understood in the dream that the baby was not hers, but the baby was her grandchild, though the mother of the baby was not there. This woman was caught up together with the baby in her arms in front of our eyes. I saw a picture of this Rapture exactly like the one below.

As I was still watching, I noticed that others were not taken, and I was one of them. Because I knew about the Rapture as a Christian, I became worried that I was not caught up. I looked up into the sky, filled with these worries, thinking what am I going to do? Discouragement came into my mind and strength left me, and I was powerless. Right there, the small voice of the HOLY SPIRIT assured me that I am only witnessing what is going to happen so that I can tell others, He assured me that I will be caught up when the time comes. That encouragement immediately gave me strength and boldness again in the dream. Another woman who was standing next to me was a tavern owner and she was left as well. This woman was so shocked, and I explained to her what was happening because at that moment I had strength. I told her that she was left because she had not received JESUS as her Lord and Savior, and the woman was helpless.

I woke up and immediately went to my sister who is a Pastor of a Pentecostal Church I had attended since birth. I explained the dream to her, and we prayed together. Because I did not want to take any responsibility for this woman's salvation (the tavern owner), after prayer, I immediately went to the woman who was not caught up. She was with a friend, and I began to witness to both of them about CHRIST and salvation.

I may not worry so much about the dreams as I said earlier that anything written in this book is like a small direction arrow pointing to the Word of God. The whole thing makes me focus on reading the Holy Bible and understanding exactly what is said in the Word. That is where 1 Thessalonians 4:16-17 comes in because sometimes GOD gives us dreams and visions so we can start to think about the real situation as it is written in His Holy Word.

The Thessalonians were wondering why many of their fellow believers had died and what would happen to them when CHRIST returned. Paul explained, as written in the above scripture, that Christians must not worry about death because there is a great hope of the resurrection of the dead when CHRIST comes. The bible says that those who are still living when the Lord returns will not meet Him ahead of those who have died. The Lord Himself will come down from heaven with a commanding shout, where the dead in CHRIST will rise first from their graves, then together with them, those who are still alive will be caught up in the clouds to meet the Lord in the air and to be with Him forever.

This precious, wonderful dream-vision captured my mind because it gave me an exciting hope about the rapture. It is important for us to know that JESUS does not force anyone to follow HIM, it is our choice whether we follow HIM or not. If we choose to follow HIM, we will be saved and receive eternal life, peace, and joy in HIM.

Our ALMIGHTY GOD is the creator of the universe. The bible begins with the majestic story of the creation of the universe, and it concludes with HIM creating a new heaven and a new earth, for the past was filled with sin. This is tremendous hope and encouragement for those who are saved in CHRIST through the HOLY SPIRIT because JESUS assures us in John 18:36 that His kingdom is not of this world. When we are with God, with our sins forgiven and our future secured, we will be made perfect like CHRIST, enjoying the eternal life in HIS kingdom which has already begun in the hearts of believers. The only entrance requirements to this magnificent place are repentance and the rebirth.

We can only live victoriously when we acknowledge the presence of the HOLY SPIRIT in us who will help us to overcome evil forces, provided we allow HIM (our main responsibilities are to allow HIM and surrender all to HIM) to lead us. And we always need to pray for courage to do what is right no matter what pressure we are faced with. The bible tells us that it is in this dispensation where we need to know that those who endure to the end and remain faithful will be rewarded by GOD. JESUS says in Revelation 3:20-22,

"Behold, I stand at the door and knock. If anyone hears My voice and opens the door, I will come into him and dine with him, and he with Me. To him who overcomes I will grant to sit with Me on My throne, as I also overcame and sat down with My Father on His throne. He, who has an ear, let him hear what the Spirit says to the churches."

Whilst I was working in New Zealand, one day I had a dream related to John 14:1-4 when JESUS was comforting HIS believers and said:-

"Do not let your hearts be troubled. You believe in God[a]; believe also in me. 2 My Father's house has many rooms; if that were not so, would I have told you that I am going there to prepare a place for you? 3 And if I go and prepare a place for you, I will come back and take you to be with me that you also may be where I am. 4 You know the way to the place where I am going."

In the dream I saw myself in the third heaven and we were in a bus. We were not many in this luxurious touring bus as we were about seven. I would say it is obvious that the bus tour driver could be an angel. I saw the streets in heaven were pure gold with beautiful grass on the sides of the street pure green. There were extremely beautiful houses or mansions but there were not the same. Most were empty but in few of them there were occupants. Our bus was not allowed to touch the golden streets, it was moving few meters up the street without touching the street. We wanted to go out and view the mansions, but we were told it is not yet the appointed time, we were not allowed to go out of the bus. Right there I saw a deceased school friend of mine whose name was Grace, but I was not allowed to talk to her. The but took us on tour until I woke up.

The primary purpose of writing this entire book is to indicate to those who have not received salvation that today is the right time to receive it as it is still available. In the book of Amos 8:12, the prophet highlights that the days are coming declared the LORD, when men will stagger from sea to sea and wander from North to East searching for the Word of the LORD. But they will not find it. Those who have received the Word of the LORD with gladness are the ones who will be Raptured. Believers are aware that the Rapture will happen anytime, and it is only GOD who knows the timing. If one is not Raptured, Revelation 6 and 7 shows that the grace of GOD will still be there since the HOLY SPIRIT will still be ministering to individual's hearts and to nations (in the absence of the Raptured Saints) for salvation, although they will receive through as martyr or being killed for the religious belief. GOD does love us including our beloved brothers and sisters that we are praying for everyday who are not yet saved, though they will see the unfolding of the tribulation events after Rapture (which includes the martyr events described under Revelation 6 and the Sealing of the 144 000 under chapter 7, including the Great Travail of Israel/ the Remnant of Judah as indicated in the book of Matthew 24, Daniel, Zachariah 10 – 14 and Revelation 6 – 19). In Revelation

14:5 we see the last Rapture of the 144 000 who are the Remnant of Judah to the Heavenly City of Jerusalem for a short while before the Second Coming of CHRIST (Hebrews 12:22). who are the Remnant of Judah.

In closing, it seems evident that all prophecies are fulfilled leading to the rapture of the saints. We read in 1 Thessalonians 4:13-18 that the Coming of the Lord is at hand and all those who believe in CHRIST – meaning all the dead from the time of creation's time and all the living – will be caught up together into the clouds to meet the Lord in the air where our bodies will be changed from perishable to imperishable (1 Corinthians 15:50-58).

You can refer to the book that I was led by the HOLY SPIRIT to write in 2014, titled "The Work of the HOLY SPIRIT Today and JESUS is Coming Book written in 2021, where most of the dreams that I had from the LORD related to the End Times are documented.

THE LEFT BEHIND

In Revelation 5, JESUS is the root of David and a Worthy Lamb to open the scrolls that were closed, HE is opening the scrolls with Authority. No one is worthy to open the scrolls except HIM alone. There is an inauguration for the Lamb by the Elders, all angels, and the Cherubim in the Throne of GOD.

In general, this section addresses the days after Rapture, when other believers are gone. We all have the beloved ones who know that we are CHRIST followers in our homes and communities. We have told them about the SAVIOR whose NAME is JESUS, who already paid the greatest price for the salvation of all individuals. The Bible says we have all sinned and fall short of the glory of GOD. In Romans 3:23, Paul extends it in general to all the world: That all the world may become guilty before GOD.

The purpose of this chapter is to show that there will still be grace after rapture because of the unfailing Love and the Grace of GOD. This evident is found in Revelation 6 where we read the following:-

"9When He opened the fifth seal, I saw under the altar the souls
of those who had been slain for the word of GOD and for the
testimony which they held. 10And they cried with a loud voice,
saying, "How long, O Lord, holy and true, until You judge and avenge
our blood on those who dwell on the earth?" 11Then a white robe was
given to each of them; and it was said to them that they should rest a
little while longer, until both the number of their fellow servants and
their brethren, who would be killed as they were, was completed."
- Revelation 6:9-11

This chapter and verses indicate that there are still saints or believers that will be saved though they will or die for the Gospel. I met a Christian woman in New Zealand who told me that she believes she will not be raptured since she is chosen to be one of the martyrs as she will be witnessing during tribulation times. She is a Christian that I respect so much, and she seems to be prepared to die for the Gospel of JESUS during the Tribulation times. We don't know GOD's plans for our future and we just surrender all unto HIM alone. In Revelation 7 we read the following:-

"9After these things I (John) looked, and behold, a great multitude
which no one could number, of all nations, tribes, peoples, and
tongues, standing before the throne and before the LAMB, clothed
with white robes, with palm branches in their hands, 10and crying
out with a loud voice, saying, "Salvation belongs to our GOD who
sits on the throne, and to the Lamb!" 11All the angels stood around
the throne and the elders and the four living creatures, and fell on
their faces before the throne and worshiped GOD, 12saying:

"Amen! Blessing and glory and wisdom,
Thanksgiving and honor and power and might,

Be to our GOD forever and ever.
Amen."

13Then one of the elders answered, saying to me, "Who
are these arrayed in white robes, and where did they
come from?" 14And I said to him, "Sir, you know."

*So, he said to me, "**These are the ones who come out of the great***
***tribulation**, and washed their robes and made them white in the*
blood of the LAMB. 15Therefore they are before the throne of
GOD and serve Him day and night in HIS temple. And HE who
sits on the throne will dwell among them. 16They shall neither
hunger anymore nor thirst anymore; the sun shall not strike
them, nor any heat; 17for the LAMB who is in the midst of the
throne will shepherd them and lead them to living fountains of
waters. And GOD will wipe away every tear from their eyes."
- Revelation 7:9-17

The hope is true because the above scriptures are written in GOD's
Word and the Word of GOD is truth, the WORD is JESUS
HIMSELF.

I would like to end this chapter by emphasizing that the Great
Tribulation believers will still be saved through Grace. As long as
they receive CHRIST as their LORD and SAVIOR, the HOLY
SPIRIT will empower them to stand on the truth even this will be
through the greatest persecution, sorrow and pain for them to die
for the Gospel since the Church Dispensation of Grace Period will
be over. Even during tribulation, their salvation will not happen
because of their power or deeds, but by HIS Grace. Without the

HOLY SPIRIT, they won't be able to stand firm persecution for the Gospel.

Those who will be saved during the tribulation of the end times after rapture must know that GOD's grace will still be with them because GOD loves them, though they will have to die for the Gospel as indicated under the book of Revelation where they are called "the martyrs".

This is the HOPE that we have in GOD as a faithful FATHER who loves HIS own children – that Grace will remain until the very end, for those of us that have chosen JESUS on time we are the chosen ones before great tribulations, and for those that will remain as the martyrs are called the Left Behind. Let us not delay in receiving Salvation until it is too late.

THE 2ND COMING
OF CHRIST

In Jude 14-15 we are told by the prophet that even Enoch also, the seventh from Adam, prophesized of these, saying behold, the LORD cometh with ten thousand of HIS saints. The prophet explain that the purpose of the LORD Second coming with saints will be to execute judgement upon all, and to convince all that are ungodly among them of all their ungodly deeds which they have ungodly committed, and of all their hard speeches which ungodly sinners have spoken against Him and to set up a kingdom that will never be broken but stand forever to eternity (Daniel 2:44-45). Those who are not HIS followers, are the ones who did not receive CHRIST as their Advocate as in John 14:6 JESUS is the only way, truth, life and the way to the FATHER no one other than HIM alone. No one comes to the Father except through Him. The prophet Zachariah in Zachariah 14:5-7, he was shown by GOD the Day of the LORD the judgement day after and GOD said:-

"...Then the Lord my GOD will come, and all the holy ones with him. On that day there will be neither sunlight nor cold, frosty darkness. It will be a unique day—a day known only to the Lord—with no distinction between day and night. When evening comes, there will be light.

In line with the above scriptures, Daniel 2:44, the prophet Daniel was shown in the dream by the LORD that during these End Times, which are the days of the kings of Psalm 83 (and all there allies) shall the GOD of heaven shall set up a kingdom, which shall never be destroyed: and this kingdom shall not be left to other people, but it shall break in pieces and consume all these kingdoms, and it shall stand forever.

It is certain that the saints will be saved from great tribulation since they will be together with CHRIST. Daniel 7:22 reveal the same, that the Ancient of the days (the LORD HIMSELF) will come, and judgement will be given to the saints of the Most High; and the time will come where the saints will possess the kingdom here on earth after Second Coming with Saints, the confirmation of Jerusalem to be the Capital City of the whole world is written in Zachariah 8:3 as the LORD said to Zachariah,

"This is what the Lord says: "I will return to Zion and dwell in Jerusalem. Then Jerusalem will be called the Faithful City, and the mountain of the Lord Almighty will be called the Holy Mountain."

That means the LORD will return to Zion and dwell in the midst of Jerusalem which shall be called the City of truth and the Holy Mountain. The tears of those who are in sorrow now will be wiped away, the streets of Jerusalem will be a safe place to play the young ones as it will be marvelous in the eyes of the Remnant and to the LORD as the LORD will serve HIS people.

Saints who are saved shall be HIS people and HE shall be our their GOD in truth and in Righteousness.

In contrary to the saints above, we read in 2 Peter 3:3-10 the following about the day of judgement to those who are not saved, Peter tells us the following:-

> "Dear friends, this is now my second letter to you. I
> have written both of them as reminders to stimulate you
> to wholesome thinking. I want you to recall the words
> spoken in the past by the holy prophets and the command
> given by our Lord and Savior through your apostles.

Above all, you must understand that in the last days scoffers will come, scoffing and following their own evil desires. They will say, "Where is this 'coming' he promised? Ever since our ancestors died, everything goes on as it has since the beginning of creation." But they deliberately forget that long ago by God's word the heavens came into being and the earth was formed out of water and by water. By these waters also the world of that time was deluged and destroyed. By the same word the present heavens and earth are reserved for fire, being kept for the day of judgment and destruction of the ungodly. But do not forget this one thing, dear friends: With the Lord a day is like a thousand years, and a thousand years are like a day. The Lord is not slow in keeping his promise, as some understand slowness. Instead he is patient with you, not wanting anyone to perish, but everyone to come to repentance. But the day of the Lord will come like a thief. The heavens will disappear with a roar; the elements will be destroyed by fire, and the earth and everything done in it will be laid bare.

In my dream of October, 2012, we were living normally, as we are today. I was living near the sea and just next to the sea was an excessively big boat made up of wood, but not fully watertight, as I could see some gaps between the timber. Amazingly, inside this boat, there was water, and I realized that this water was not leaking in spite of the gaps between the wood. It came to my mind that it must be GOD who was holding this water in the boat. As I explored the boat with some others, we were told that everyone must run into a big church building nearby for safety because the water in the boat will be released. Many were far away, and did not hear the message, but we ran into the church building. When we entered the church, the door of the church was closed behind us. The water of the boat was then released and flooded the whole earth. All people who were not inside the church died whilst we watched from the church windows – though the height of this water outside was well above the church windows. We had to wait for days until the water dried up.

After some days, we went outside and began a new life again, and the population grew. During that time, I was not living near the sea, but I was living near the same church building which this time was situated in the Middle East. In the dream, I knew it was situated near the center of the earth. I was aware that the LORD JESUS was there as well, though I couldn't see HIM literally. HE was in authority over the whole earth, not just the Middle East. As people were busy doing their day-to-day things, we were told that we needed to run to the church again for safety, which we did. Many of us were thinking about our relatives who were far away and who did not hear the message so they could be saved as well, but it was too late. We then entered this church building which had an open hall without any dividing walls. Our purpose was to do nothing, except to be saved. After the door was closed, fire came from heaven and I really sensed a pull from my spirit that the LORD was there and in authority to destroy all evil, keeping us safe in the church. This fire covered the whole earth and consumed all living things and elements that were on the earth as we watched again from the church and were not affected by this fire at all.

After some days, quietness came and there was no fire anymore. This time, we did not go out of the church as we had after the floods but the church developed walls inside and it became like a city where we all began to establish our lives. The church roof disappeared, and a new environment was felt with freedom, security, and quietness in a brotherly-spirit environment. I saw the sun coming through from the sky into this new city and there was light all over without any darkness just before I woke up.

My dream concluded with a picture of the holy city – a New Jerusalem. I encourage you to read scriptures from Revelation 21-22 on this topic. Above all, it should be noted that I was just a witness in all the dreams I have highlighted in this book so I could tell others. I did nothing except to witness.

In conclusion, the Kingdom of GOD will be fully realized when CHRIST comes back again as the KING of KINGS to destroy the kingdom of darkness forever and literally establish and reign in HIS Kingdom that will stand forever here on earth.

ACKNOWLEDGMENTS

I want to thank GOD for the men and women, known to the HOLY SPIRIT, who were praying for me and my family during the writing of the three books 1.The work of the HOLY SPIRIT TODAY THE END TIMES 2.JESUS is coming 3.The Raptured Saints and the left behind. Not forgetting all members of "JESUS is Coming Ministry" who stood by me on prayers and to minister in Africa. Acknowledgements also goes to Kate Delaney (America Tonight) and Dr Angela Budd Chester who assisted to spread the message of my previous two books not limited to America, Canada, UK, Philippians, Australia and New Zealand through their TV shows, Radio Broadcasts, podcast, News Papers etc. I won't forget Saffron Brown (from USA) who was my assistant

I would also like to thank my son Brian Mxolisi Radebe who also stood by my side no matter what since from the conception of the divine dreams whilst we were still overseas. Not forgetting all family members who were always there for me on prayers.

It was not easy but I do see the Will of GOD happening as I yield to the HOLY SPIRIT. Most importantly, I must thank GOD for my deceased mother Esther Radebe who raised us under the Christian teachings and also acknowledge the encouragement coming from my deceased dad, who was an Author.

GOD uses individuals with different talents to accomplish HIS Work – to write, read, edit, design covers, pray, encourage, etc. since the salvation Work is not ours, but the Work of the HOLY SPIRIT.

According to the book of Numbers 6:24-27

To the reader of this book:-May the LORD bless you and keep you, May the LORD make HIS Face shine upon you, and may HE be gracious to you, May the LORD lift up HIS countenance upon you and give you peace. I say all of this in JESUS NAME. Amen

ABOUT THE AUTHOR

Isabel Nodoli Radebe was is blessed with one son and was brought up in a Pentecostal Christian family in South Africa; however, she began to have more knowledge about the HOLY SPIRIT in 2004. At the age of twelve in 1983, a man of God, who was sent by God, told her that after time, GOD will send her to a very remotest country, and she took it lightly, because she was young at that time. This man of GOD died years after the message, and this prophecy in her life was fulfilled after twenty-three years when she found herself working in New Zealand, which was never in her mind before. She lived and worked in New Zealand as a Civil Engineer for five years where she received a lot of divine dreams and came back to South Africa in December 2010.

Like many other men and women who went through trials of life though at the end, GOD used her to start the End Times Ministry known as "JESUS is Coming Ministry" which together with the members have reached out to many nations also through her two previous books she wrote titled, "The Work of the HOLY SPIRIT Today the End Times and JESUS is Coming".

Through writing of this book, she thank GOD the HOLY SPIRIT for using her as the vessel to reach out to many souls.